Honeycomb

William K. Durr
Jean M. LePere
Mary Lou Alsin
Ruth Patterson Bunyan
Susan Shaw

CONSULTANT Paul McKee

HOUGHTON MIFFLIN COMPANY • Boston

Atlanta • Dallas • Geneva, Illinois • Hopewell, New Jersey • Palo Alto • Toronto

Acknowledgments

For each of the selections listed below, grateful acknowledgement is made for permission to adapt and/or reprint copyrighted material, as follows:

"Bees," by Jack Prelutsky. Reprinted with permission of Macmillan Publishing Co., Inc. from *Toucans Two and Other Poems* by Jack Prelutsky. Copyright © 1967, 1970 by Jack Prelutsky. British rights granted by Hamish Hamilton Children's Books Ltd.

"Buzzy Bear and the Rainbow." From *Buzzy Bear and the Rainbow* by Dorothy Marino, copyright © 1962 by Franklin Watts, Inc.

"Cookies," from *Frog and Toad Together* by Arnold Lobel. Copyright © 1972 by Arnold Lobel. Reprinted by permission of Harper & Row, Publishers, Inc. British rights granted by World's Work Ltd.

"Ira Sleeps Over," by Bernard Waber. Copyright © 1972 by Bernard Waber. Reprinted by permission of Houghton Mifflin Company.

"The Little Raccoon," by Jim Wells. Reprinted from *Ranger Rick's Nature Magazine* by permission of the publisher, the National Wildlife Federation.

"Little Raccoon and the Thing in the Pool." Adapted from *Little Raccoon and the Thing in the Pool*, by Lilian Moore. Pictures by Gioia Fiammenghi. Copyright © 1963 by Lilian Moore and Gioia Fiammenghi. Used with permission of McGraw-Hill Book Co.

"My Dog Is a Plumber," by Dan Greenburg. From *Free to Be . . . You And Me*, by Marlo Thomas, et al., published by McGraw-Hill Book Company and the Ms. Foundation, Inc. Copyright © 1974 Free To Be Foundation Inc.

"Off for a Hike," by Aileen Fisher. From *Feathered Ones and Furry* by Aileen Fisher. Copyright © 1971 by Aileen Fisher, with permission of Thomas Y. Crowell Company, Inc., publisher.

"What Is It?" by Beatrice Schenk de Regniers. "Elephant" and "Frog" from *It Does Not Say Meow*, by Beatrice Schenk de Regniers, copyright © 1972 by the author and reprinted by permission of The Seabury Press, Inc.

Illustrators: pp. 7–21, TRINA SCHART HYMAN; pp. 22–27, JOSEPH MATHIEU; pp. 28–45, BILL CHARMATZ; pp. 46–64, LINDA BOEHM; pp. 65–78, ED EMBERLEY; pp. 79–80, JOSEPH MATHIEU; pp. 81–82, MARC BROWN; pp. 85–112, BERNARD WABER; pp. 113–117, JERRY PINKNEY; pp. 118–119, DEE ANNE DYKE; pp. 120–140, MONICA ANAGNOSTARAS; pp. 141–143, JOSEPH MATHIEU; p. 144, OLIVIA COLE; pp. 145–146, MARC BROWN; pp. 147–162, DAVID MCPHAIL; p. 165, JON PROVEST; pp. 166–191, JOE VENO; pp. 192–194, JOSEPH MATHIEU; p. 195, LADY MCCRADY; pp. 196–197, MERYL ROSNER; pp. 198–208, ARNOLD LOBEL.

Photographers: p. 113, BILL SUMNER; p. 114, OWEN FRANKEN/STOCK BOSTON, INC.; pp. 115–116, BILL SUMNER; p. 117, AT&T PHOTO CENTER and NEW ENGLAND TELEPHONE.

Book cover, title page, and magazine covers by TOM UPSHUR

Contents

Ripples

Ripples

6

Joe: Do you know what I have in here?

Steve: Is it a toy?

Is it something funny?

Joe: It's not really funny.

But I have a lot of fun with it.

Take a look!

Steve: I thought you had a toy in there.

But it's a real frog.

Where did you get it?

Joe: It's not a real frog.

It's a little toy!

I got it at the toy store.

Steve: Your toy frog will be a lot of fun.

It looks just like a real one.

Joe: I just thought of something, Steve.

We can go find Betty and Sue.

And we can scare them with this frog.

Come on!

Joe: Hi, Betty.

I have a surprise in here.

I got it at the toy store.

Betty: I like toys!

Will you let me see it?

Joe: She thought it was a real frog.

Steve: That was fun!

She's going to Sue's house now.

She will tell Sue it's a real frog.

Joe: Let's put the frog back in here.

We can really have some fun now.

Joe: Hi, girls.

What are you doing?

Can we come in?

Betty: No, you two boys can't come in.

You have that frog.

And we don't want any frogs in here.

Steve: What frog?

You don't see any frogs, do you?

Sue: No, we don't see any frogs.

But we just don't want you to come in.

Steve: I know what we can do.

Sh! Don't make any noise.

We can't go in there.

But the frog can.

Joe: I thought of doing that.

The girls don't like frogs.

Betty: Sue! It's that frog!

Get it away from here.

Sue: This is just a toy frog.

And I'm not scared of real frogs.

All they can do is jump.

Betty: Steve and Joe surprised me.

That wasn't a nice thing to do.

Sue: I know what we can do, Betty.

The boys will want this frog back.

Then they will get a surprise.

Come with me!

We'll get something from my house.

Betty: This is going to be fun.

Now we can scare Joe and Steve!

Wait and see how they run!

Sue: Hi, Joe. Hi, Steve.

Are you looking for something?

Steve: Yes, we're looking for Joe's frog.

Is it in that box?

Joe: My toy frog scared you, didn't it?

You thought it was a real one.

Betty: It really did surprise me.

Sue: Here's the box.

Steve: Let's open it, Joe.

Is the frog in there?

Betty: Yes, there's a frog in the box.

We don't want your frog.

It's a real frog!

Betty: Come back! Come back!

Don't you want your toy frog?

Sue: How do you like being scared?

Joe: I wasn't really scared.

Just a little surprised.

I'm not scared of frogs.

Betty: Not much!

How Do You Know?

 Look what I have.

How do you know the girl said this?

The little picture tells you.

| Maria: | Look what I have. |

How do you know the girl said this?

The girl's name tells you.

Maria said, "Look what I have."

How do you know the girl said this?

The words **Maria said** tell you.

How do you know what she said?

Now read this story.

Can you tell who said what?

Maria said, "Look at this."

David said, "I like it."

"Put it on," David said.

"No, I don't want to," Maria said.

"I can help you put it on," said David.

"I know how," said Maria.

"But I don't want to."

"It's a good hat," said David.

"I know it's a good hat," said Maria.

"I like it."

"Then put it on!" David said.

"I won't put this hat on!" said Maria.

"Then, can I put it on?" David asked.

"You won't like it," Maria said.

"Can I put it on anyway?" asked David.

"Here it is, David," said Maria.

"It's so big!" said David.

"That's the problem," said Maria.

"It's a good hat, anyway!" said David.

CAN A MOUSE REALLY HELP?

Mouse was not happy.

"No one will play with me," said Mouse.

29

"Hi, Rabbit!" said Mouse.

"Can you play?"

"No," said Rabbit.

"I want to see how far I can jump.

You'll get in my way.

You're too little.

Go away, Mouse."

"Wait, Squirrel!" said Mouse.

"Where are you going?"

"I have to go to work," Squirrel said.

"I could help you," said Mouse.

"You couldn't help me," said Squirrel.
"You're too little."

"You aren't <u>that</u> big, you know,"
said Mouse.

"I don't want to be seen
with a mouse," said Squirrel.

"I'm scared of Tiger," said Mouse.

"I'm getting out of here."

"Help! Help!" cried Mouse.

"Tiger will get me!"

"What's that noise?" asked Lion.

"It's me!" said Mouse.

"Tiger is after me!"

"Are you going to eat me up?"
asked Mouse.

"No, I won't eat you," said Lion.
"I had my lunch."

"Did Tiger eat lunch?" asked Mouse.

"I don't know," Lion said.

"I'm scared!" cried Mouse.
"Will you help me?"

"What will you do if I help you?"
asked Lion.

"If you help me, some day
I'll help you," said Mouse.

"What? A mouse can't help a lion!"
said Lion.

"That's funny!"

Lion laughed and laughed.

"I have to go now," said Mouse.

35

"I'm lucky Tiger didn't get me,"

Mouse said.

"And I'm lucky I got away from Lion.

She was too busy laughing to get me."

"Do you know what that little mouse did today?" asked Lion.

"Yes," said Tiger.
"He ran into me!"

"Then he ran to me for help!" Lion said.

"I think that's funny!" said Tiger.

"You think <u>that's</u> funny!"
Lion said.

"Then Mouse said he could help me
some day."

"How can a mouse help a lion!"
said Tiger.

"That's very funny!"
Tiger laughed.

"It's very, very funny!"
said Lion.

Lion laughed and laughed.

She didn't look where she was going.

"Look out!" cried Tiger.

"Help!" cried Lion.

"I'm coming!" said Tiger.

"I'll get you out!"

"I can't do it!" said Tiger.

"I'll have to get some help.

Wait for me here, Lion."

"I'll have to," said Lion.

She was scared.

"Come and help Lion!" cried Tiger.

"Help get her out!"

"Can't you see I'm busy!"
said Squirrel.

"I don't have time to help.

You're big, Tiger.

You get her out."

"I can't do it without help,"
said Tiger.

"Come on!

We'll get Rabbit to help, too."

41

"We can't do it," said Tiger.

"It won't work," said Squirrel.

"We can't get her out," said Rabbit.

"What's going on?" asked Mouse.

"We can't get Lion out of here," said Rabbit.

"I can help!" said Mouse.

"Go away," said Squirrel.
"You'll just be in the way."

"I want to help," said Mouse.

"How can you help?" Rabbit asked.

"Let me think!" said Mouse.

"I've got it!" cried Mouse.
"I know what to do!"

"What?" asked Tiger.

"I'll make a hole in it.
Then we can get Lion out."

43

"Look at that!" said Tiger.

"He's doing it!" said Squirrel.

"Now, help me get her out,"
said Mouse.

All the animals helped.

"I'm out!" Lion cried.

"We did it! We did it!"
cried all the animals.

"Mouse is the one who did it,"
said Lion.

"Who helps me if I want help?"
cried Lion.

"We all help!" said Mouse.

"But who is the biggest help?"
cried Lion.

All of the animals cried,
"Mouse is the biggest help!"

This time no one laughed.

Lucy Didn't Listen

Lucy was a busy worker.

She painted a lot of nice pictures.

She was a good reader.

And she liked to put things away.

But Lucy had one problem.

She did not listen.

One day Lucy was busy painting.

Mrs. Day said, "Put your work away.
We have to go to the library now."

But Lucy didn't listen.
She was too busy painting.

Lucy looked up from the painting.

She saw the boys and girls going out.

"I'll have to stop painting," she thought.

"We are going to lunch now.

I'll get my lunch."

Mary saw Lucy with her lunch bag.

"What are you doing with that?" she said.

"Are your library books in there?"

"No," said Lucy.

"I thought we were going to lunch."

Mrs. Day looked at Lucy and said,
"Oh, Lucy! You didn't listen.
I said that we were going to the library."

Lucy said, "I do listen, Mrs. Day.
Today I was too busy painting.
I didn't hear you."

"You'll have to go back to the room,"
said Mrs. Day.
"Get your library book.
Then come to the library."

51

Mary saw Lucy come into the library.

Lucy had her book and her lunch bag.

"You didn't put your lunch bag away,"
said Mary.

"I was much too busy getting my book,"
said Lucy.

Lucy looked for a good book to read.

She wanted a book about animals.

"Do you all have your books now?"
said Mrs. Day.

"Yes, Mrs. Day," said all the children
but Lucy.

Lucy didn't hear Mrs. Day.

She was too busy reading her book.

"After we get back to the room,
we'll go out to play," said Mrs. Day.

Jim said, "Lucy's back in the library.
She was reading when I saw her.
Do you want me to get her?"

"Yes, please. Tell her to come with us,"
said Mrs. Day.

Jim went to get Lucy.

When she and Jim got back to the room,
the children were going out.

Lucy and Jim went out, too.

Lucy had her lunch bag and her book.

"Did you forget to put
your things away?" said Charlie.

But Lucy didn't hear him.
She was too busy reading a story.

Lucy was busy reading when Mary said,

"Let's play SQUIRREL IN THE TREE."

Jim went over to Lucy and said,

"Come on, Lucy.

Please be a squirrel in this tree."

He put Lucy with two children.

Then Mrs. Day said,

"Run, squirrels, run!"

But Lucy didn't run.

Charlie said, "Run, Lucy, run!

Please listen, will you?

Run to that tree over there!"

"I'm listening," said Lucy.

"I can run over to that tree."

And she did!

Mary looked over at Lucy.

"Oh, Lucy!" she said.

"You didn't listen at all.

We didn't want you to run

to the real tree!"

The children had fun playing.

When the time for play was over,

they went back to their room to work.

Then Mrs. Day said,

"We're going to Room 2.

We will see a puppet play there.

Please put your work away now."

But where was Lucy?

In the workroom!

She was putting her things away.

She didn't hear what Mrs. Day said.

After Lucy had put the things away,

she went back into the big room.

"No one is here," she thought.

"Where did the others go?

They didn't go out to play.

And they didn't go to the library.

I know! They went to eat their lunch!

I'll get my lunch bag!"

Lucy went to the lunchroom.

But the others were not there.

"Where could they all be?"
thought Lucy.

"It can't be time to eat now.

I'll have to go back to the room.

They all went somewhere without me."

Lucy went back to her room.

"I don't know what to do now,"
thought Lucy.

"I'm scared in this big room."

Just then Mrs. Day walked in.

"Here you are, Lucy!" she said.

"I have looked and looked for you.

I couldn't find you."

"I thought you were eating.

Where were you?" said Lucy.

"I said that we were going

to a puppet play," said Mrs. Day.

"Oh, good!" said Lucy.

"I like plays!"

"You may not get to see the play, Lucy.

It may be all over," said Mrs. Day.

Lucy and Mrs. Day went to Room 2.

"Oh, my!" said Lucy.

"Is this the end?"

"You weren't listening, Lucy,"
said Mrs. Day.

"And you didn't get to see the play.

It was a play about goats."

"I couldn't hear you.

I was busy in the workroom," said Lucy.

"I had to put my things away."

"You are a good worker, Lucy,"
said Mrs. Day.

"But you can have more fun
if you listen."

"I'm not going to be too busy
to listen any more!" said Lucy.

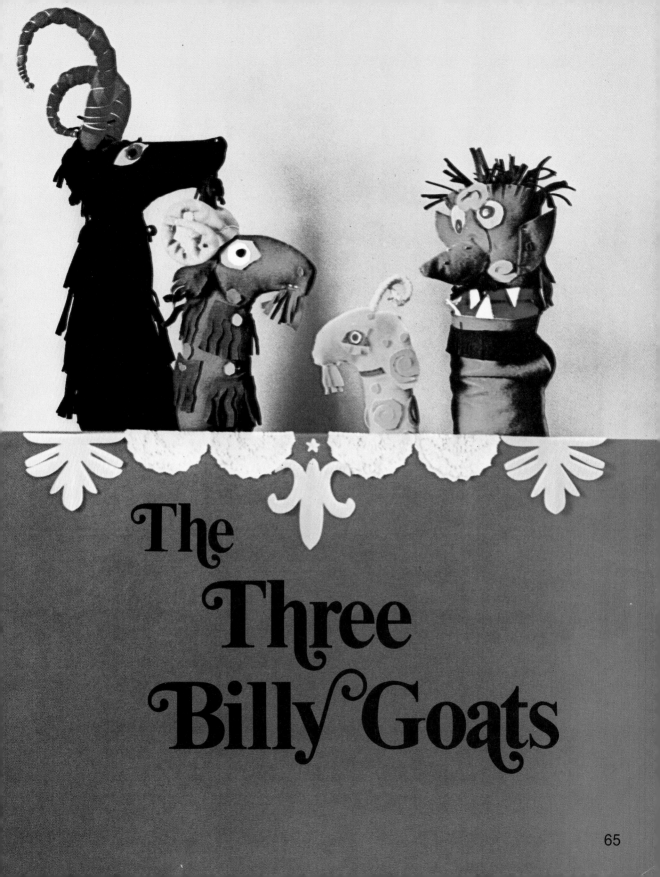

The Three Billy Goats

You are going to read a play
about three billy goats.

You can make puppets for this play.

Make a big, big puppet to be
Big, Big Billy Goat.

Make a big puppet to be
Big Billy Goat.

Make a little puppet to be
Little Billy Goat.

Make a scary-looking puppet to be
the troll.

The mean troll may have big teeth
for eating billy goats!

You can make a bridge.

The bridge will hide the troll.

The goats will go over the bridge.

Have someone be the noisemaker.

The noisemaker will make

the foot noises for the billy goats

on the bridge.

TROLL'S
BRIDGE

THE PLAY

TROLL: I am a mean troll.

And this is my bridge.

I'm happy to have you here.

You can come onto my bridge

any time you want.

But when you do, I'll eat you up!

Ha, ha, ha!

LITTLE BILLY GOAT: Oh, I see

some nice green grass over there.

I'll just go over that bridge

and get some.

NOISEMAKER: (MAKE LITTLE FOOT NOISES.)

TROLL: What's all that noise on my bridge?

LITTLE BILLY GOAT: It's Little Billy Goat.

I'm going to get some nice green grass.

It's on that hillside over there.

TROLL: When you go over my bridge,

I'll eat you up!

I'm a mean troll! Ha, ha, ha!

LITTLE BILLY GOAT: Oh, no! I'm too little

to eat.

Wait for Big Billy Goat.

He will want some of that grass.

He'll be coming over your bridge.

TROLL: Get out of here, then,

before I eat the two of you.

NOISEMAKER: (MAKE LITTLE FOOT NOISES.)

BIG BILLY GOAT: Oh, Little Billy Goat

is eating on that hillside.

The grass looks better over there.

I want some before he eats it all.

NOISEMAKER: (MAKE BIG FOOT NOISES.)

TROLL: What's making that noise on my bridge?

BIG BILLY GOAT: I am Big Billy Goat. I'm going to the hillside.

TROLL: I've waited and waited for you. Ha, ha, ha! You'll make a nice big lunch for me.

BIG BILLY GOAT: Oh, no!

Don't eat me up.

I'm not very big.

But Big, Big Billy Goat is on his way.

And I can hear him coming.

TROLL: Then get away from here
before I put an end to you.

NOISEMAKER: (MAKE BIG FOOT NOISES.)

BIG, BIG BILLY GOAT: Oh, my!

Little Billy Goat and Big Billy Goat

are eating that nice green grass.

I want some, too.

NOISEMAKER: (MAKE BIG, BIG FOOT NOISES.)

TROLL: What's all that noise up there?

BIG, BIG BILLY GOAT: I'm

Big, Big Billy Goat.

I'm going to that hillside

to get some nice green grass.

TROLL: Oh, no, you're not.

I've waited and waited for you.

I'm going to eat you up!

BIG, BIG BILLY GOAT: Get out
of my way, you old troll!
You didn't eat Little Billy Goat.
You didn't eat Big Billy Goat.
And you're not going to eat me!

TROLL: I let the two of them go.
I was waiting for a big lunch!
And you're it!

BIG, BIG BILLY GOAT: Take that!

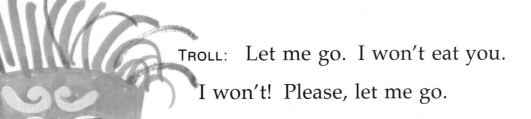

TROLL: Let me go. I won't eat you.
I won't! Please, let me go.

BIG, BIG BILLY GOAT: That's more like it.
You get away from here now.

TROLL: But I can't go away.
This bridge is my home.

BIG, BIG BILLY GOAT: It's my bridge now.
You go find another bridge.
And don't come back here.

77

BIG, BIG BILLY GOAT: I'm a big, big old
billy goat.

You can come onto my bridge
any time you want.

And—

I won't eat you up!

One Word from Two Words

Sometimes you will see a word

that is made of two words you know.

You know the word **play,** and you know

the word **house.**

Now you can read the word **playhouse.**

What two words make the word **doghouse?**

Here are more words made

from two words you know.

The words here are made

with the word **any** and one other word.

We didn't have **anyone** to play with.

We didn't have **anything** to do.

We didn't have **anywhere** to go.

ANYWAY, IT ALL WORKED OUT.

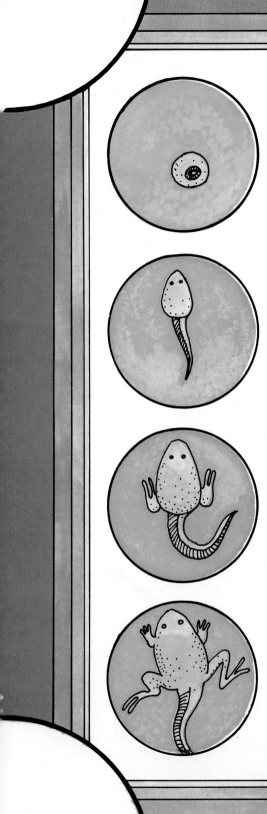

WHAT IS IT?

by Beatrice Schenk de Regniers

When it is born
It is all head and tail
    — mostly tail.
You could keep it at home
In a tub or a pail
    — a very small pail.

When it's grown up
It has no more tail.
Hoppity hop,
It jumps out of the pail.

Now it swims in a pond
Or hops on dry land.
Catches flies with its tongue
And sings a loud song,
Ka-ga-lunk **or** *Ka-chug,*
As it sits on a log.
It's a . . .

Waves

Waves

WHAT WILL YOU BE?

What do you want to be
when you grow up?

You may want to be a . . .

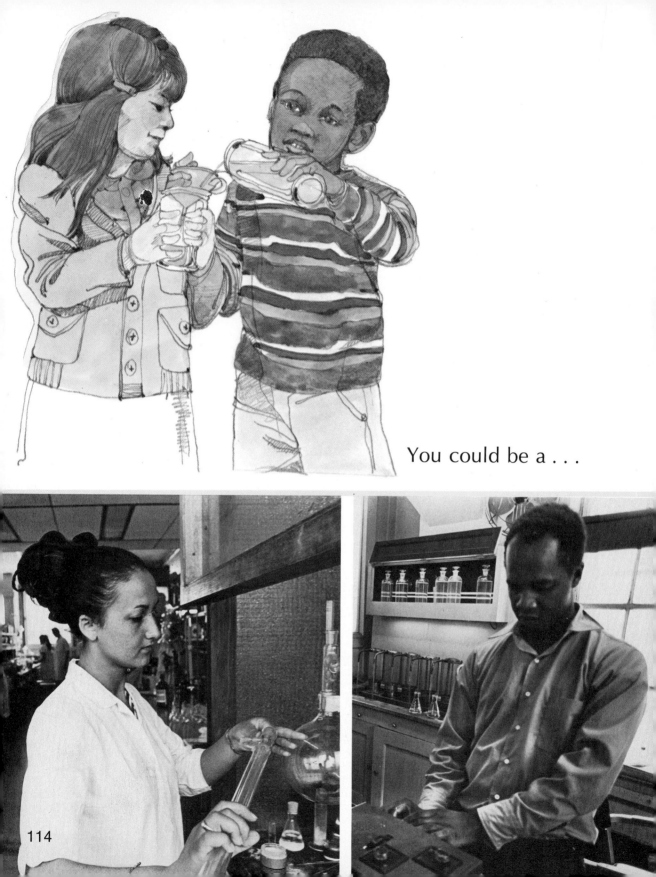

You could be a . . .

Maybe you'll want to be a . . .

You may decide to be a . . .

What other things could you be

when you grow up?

My Dog Is a Plumber

My dog is a plumber,

he must be a boy.

Although I must tell you

his favorite toy

Is a little play stove

with pans and with pots

Which he really must like,

'cause he plays with it lots.

So perhaps he's a girl,

    which kind of makes sense,

Since he can't throw a ball

    and he can't climb a fence.

But neither can Dad,

    and I know *he's* a man,

And Mom is a woman,

    and *she* drives a van.

Maybe the problem is

    in trying to tell

Just what someone is

    by what he does well.

— *Dan Greenburg*

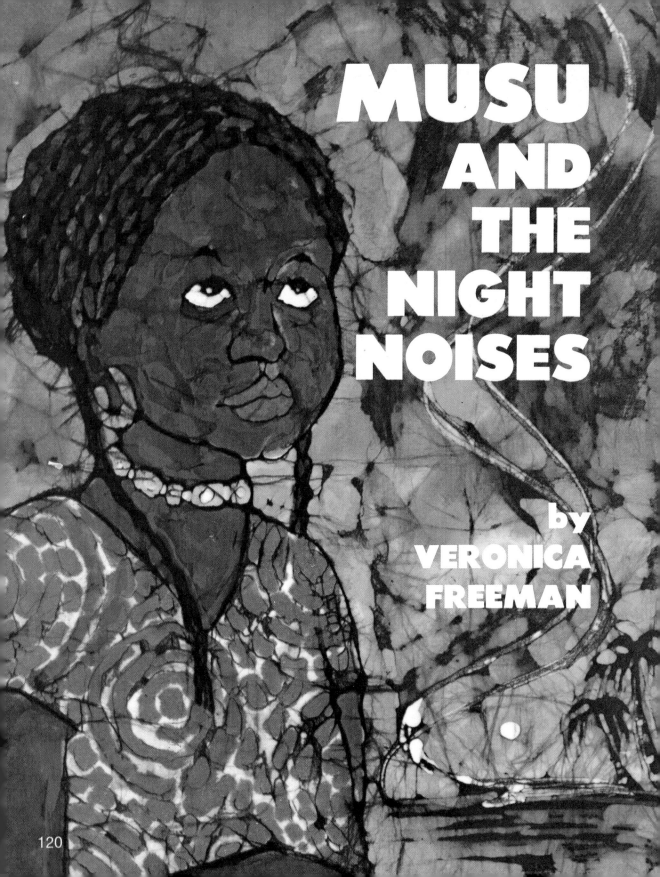

MUSU AND THE NIGHT NOISES

by
VERONICA
FREEMAN

Musu looked away to the water.

"Is it time for the fish to come in?"
she asked her mother.

"I'll tell you when we should go,"
Musu's mother said.

After some time, Musu's mother said,
"We can go down to the water now."

Musu and her mother walked down
to the water.
There were others there.
They were waiting for the fish
to come in, too.
Zoe was there with her mother.
Zoe was Musu's friend.

"We'll wait here," said Musu's mother.

"Will Father let me help today?"
Musu asked.

"He may," her mother said.

"You can ask him when he gets here."

"There they are!" cried Musu.

"There are the men coming in
with the fish!"

She jumped up and ran to the water.

Musu's father was bigger than any
of the other men.

Musu could see his big smile.

Now Musu ran to her father.

"May I help with the fish?"
she asked.

"You may," said her father.
"We need a lot of help.
We were lucky today.
We have many, many fish."

Musu helped the others take the fish
to the big pans.

Everyone worked and worked.

It was night by the time all the fish
were in the pans.

"Did you ever see so many fish?"
asked Musu.

"We got more fish today
than we ever got before,"
said Musu's father.

"We can't take all these fish
back with us," said Musu's mother.
"What will we do with the ones
we can't take back?"

"Someone will have to stay here
to look after them," said Musu's father.

"Please let me stay!" cried Musu,
jumping up and down.

"You can't stay here by yourself,
Musu," said her father.

"Zoe, you'll stay with me,
won't you?" asked Musu.

"Yes," said Zoe.
"Musu and I will take good care
of the fish."

Zoe's mother said she could stay.

"We'll be right back,"
said Musu's father.

"Now be very careful."

"Just look at that moon," said Zoe.

"It's really bright."

"That's good," said Musu.

"If anyone comes to take these fish,
we'll see who it is."

After some time, Zoe said,
"The others should be back by now.
Where can they be?"

"Zoe, you must go and find out
where they are," said Musu.
"I'll stay with the fish."

"No, you must not stay
by yourself," said Zoe.
"It's scary down here,
even if the moon is bright."

There were many noises.

Musu's mother called them
night noises.

"Listen very carefully in the daytime,"
her mother had said.

"You won't hear the noises
you hear at night."

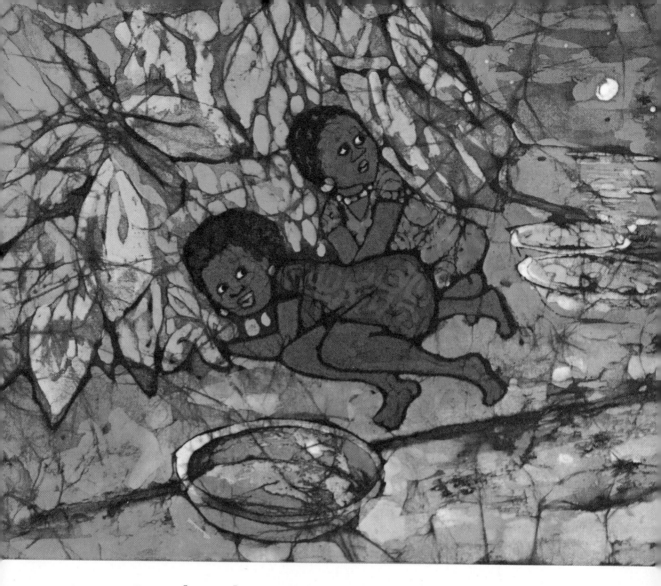

Just then there was a loud noise.

It wasn't like any of the night noises.

"Someone is coming to take the fish."
said Musu.

"Let's hide in here."

Musu looked out of the hideout.

She saw some boys looking at the fish.

Musu couldn't tell who the boys were.

"Look how many pans they left!"
one boy said.

"They're taking the fish," said Zoe.

"We've got to do something!"

"Sh, I know what to do!" said Musu.

Musu saw the stick her father had left.

It was just outside the hideout.

Musu picked up the stick.

She began to make noises with it.

"What's that?" asked one boy.

"Don't be scared," said another boy.

"That's just a night noise.

Night noises can't do anything."

"That didn't even scare the boys
a little!" said Zoe.

"They think it was just a night noise."

"They'll soon hear what night noises
can do," said Musu.

"Get that pan, Zoe."

Zoe picked up a big fish pan.

Musu took the stick.

BANG! BANG! BANG!

The girls made a lot of loud noises.

"Let's get out of here!"
shouted the boys.

"Let the fish stay!"

"I don't think they'll come back
after this," said Musu.

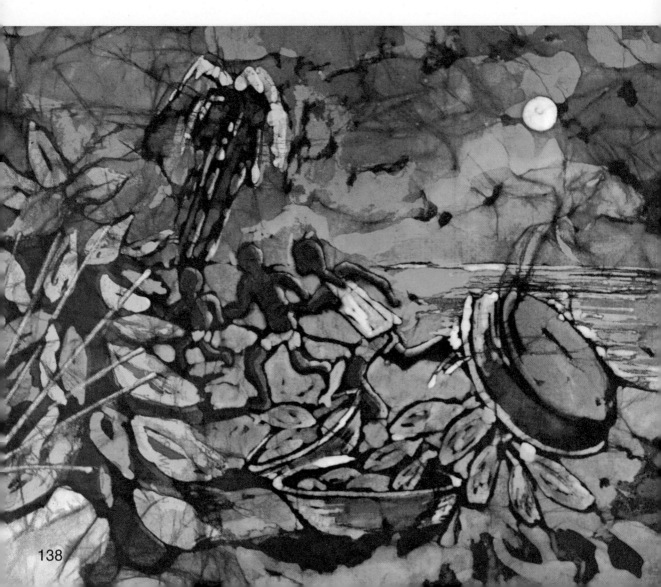

"Sh, I hear more noises," said Zoe.

"Get the pan!" said Musu.
"They won't get these fish!"

BANG! BANG! BANG!

"Musu! Zoe! Is that you?"
shouted Musu's father.

"Is that you, Father?"
called Musu.

"You scared us, Musu,"
said her father.

"And you scared the boys, too.

I asked them to come for the fish.

But I forgot to tell them

about you two."

"What the girls did was good,"
said one of the boys.

"They really took care of the fish!"

Inside Out

Mother Dog and Father Dog had
two little dogs named Out and In.

"It is time for bed," said Mother Dog.
"Where are Out and In?"

"Out is in and In is out,"
said Father Dog.

"No, I am in," said In.

"It is Out who is out."

"In, please go out and bring Out in,"
said Mother Dog.

As soon as In was out,
Out came in.

"Now Out is in, and In is out!"
said Father Dog.

"I'll get In," said Out.

"You are in," said Father Dog.

"It is In who is out!"

"I am Out and I am in," said Out.

"But I, Out, am going out

to get In in."

"It is all too much for me,"

said Father Dog.

Where was In at the end of the story?

Where was Out?

BEES

Every bee

that

ever was

was

partly

sting

and partly

. . . buzz.

— *Jack Prelutsky*

WHAT IS IT?

by Beatrice Schenk de Regniers

A short short tail.

A long long nose

He uses for

A water hose.

Two great big ears.

Four great big feet.

A tiny peanut

Is a treat for him.

His name is El —

Oh no! I can't!

Now you tell me:

An . . .

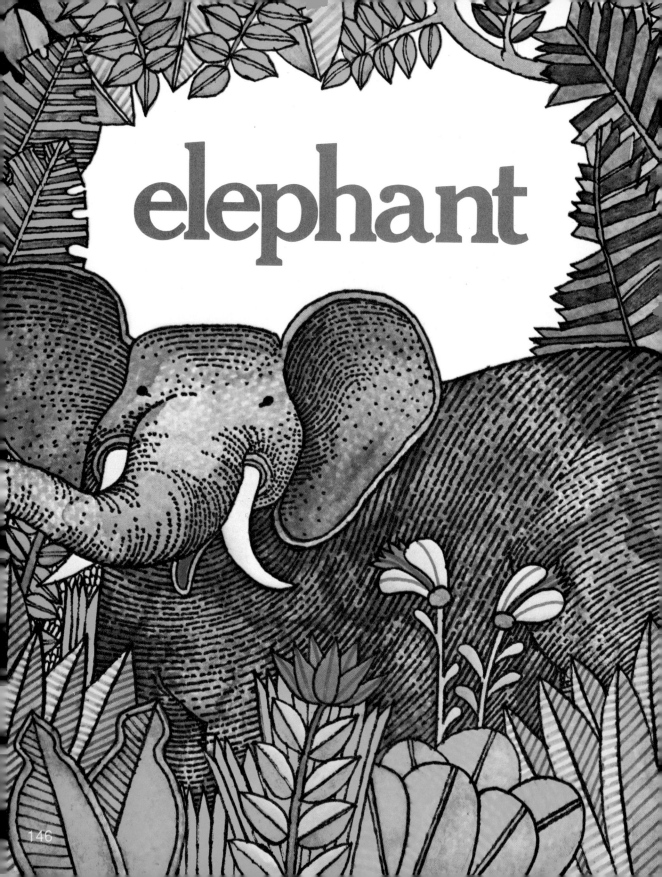

elephant

BUZZY BEAR
and the
RAINBOW

BY

DOROTHY MARINO

One day Buzzy Bear ran out to play.

It had just stopped raining.

Buzzy stopped by a tree.

"Oh, look!" he cried to a bird

in a tree.

"There's a rainbow."

"Yes, I know," said the bird.

"They say there's gold at the end
of the rainbow.

But you have to get there
before it goes away."

Buzzy didn't wait to hear more.

He ran home.

Mother and Father Bear were looking
at the rainbow, too.

CORN   BEANS   PEAS   MARSH-MALLOWS   BUBBLE GUM

149

Buzzy ran into the house
to get a big pot.

When he had come back out, he said,
"I'm going to get the gold."
Then he ran on.

"That's just a story,"
called Mother Bear.

"Gold would not do us any good,"
called Father Bear.

Buzzy just ran on.

He could see the end of the rainbow

by a big rock.

When Buzzy got to the big rock,

he couldn't see the rainbow.

A squirrel was there.

"I'm looking for the end

of the rainbow," said Buzzy

to the squirrel.

"Look at the bushes over there,"

said the squirrel.

"There's the end of the rainbow."

Buzzy ran to find it.

The squirrel called after him,
"If you're looking for the gold,
that's just a story."

Buzzy just ran on.
When he got to the bushes,
he couldn't see the rainbow.
A rabbit was there.

"I'm trying to find the end
of the rainbow," said Buzzy
to the rabbit.

152

"See that grass over there?"
the rabbit said.

"There's the end of the rainbow."

Buzzy ran to find it.

The rabbit called after him,
"If you're looking for the gold,
that's just a story."

Buzzy just ran on.
When he got to the grass,
he couldn't see the rainbow.
A chipmunk was there.

153

"I'm trying to find the end
of the rainbow," said Buzzy
to the chipmunk.

"Look at that high tree over there,"
said the chipmunk.
"There's the end of the rainbow."

Buzzy ran to find it.
The chipmunk called after him,
"If you're looking for the gold,
that's just a story."
Buzzy just ran on.

When he got to the tree,

Buzzy looked all over.

There was no rainbow anywhere.

"This really must be the end

of the rainbow!" said Buzzy.

"I wonder if I got here in time."

155

Buzzy went up the tree.

Then he stopped.

There was a big hole in the tree.

Buzzy looked in.

"I've found it," he cried.

He took a mouthful.

"I found the gold . . . and I like it."

Buzzy put the gold into the big pot.

Then he climbed down the tree.

"I'll run home now," thought Buzzy.

"I found the gold," Buzzy called
to the chipmunk as he ran by the grass.

"Wait, let me see," cried the chipmunk.

Buzzy just ran on.

The chipmunk ran after Buzzy.

"I found the gold," Buzzy called
to the rabbit as he ran by the bushes.

"Wait, let me see," cried the rabbit.

Buzzy just ran on ahead.

The rabbit ran after Buzzy

and the chipmunk.

"I found the gold," Buzzy called
to the squirrel as he ran
by the big rock.

"Wait, let me see," cried the squirrel.

Buzzy just ran on ahead.

The squirrel ran after Buzzy
and the chipmunk and the rabbit.

159

They all ran to Buzzy's house.

Buzzy Bear put the big pot down.

"Look, Mother," he cried.

"There really was gold at the end
of the rainbow.

I ate some."

They all looked into the pot.

"It's honey!" cried Father Bear.

"Buzzy found honey at the end
of the rainbow!"

Buzzy Bear called the little bird
from the tree.

Then Mother Bear asked all the animals
to eat supper with them.

161

Mother Bear made pancakes.

They put the golden honey on them.

My, they tasted good.

"I'm happy Buzzy looked for the gold,"
said Mother Bear.

And Father Bear said,
"The gold that Buzzy found
is better than real gold!"

Pools

Pools

The Little Raccoon

The little raccoon

Looked at the moon

From his home in the old hollow tree;

The wind, warm and light,

Blew soft in the night

And the woods were as still as could be.

The little raccoon

Smiled back at the moon,

For contented and happy was he;

The woodsman that day

Had seen him at play

And his axe never touched the old tree.

— *Jim Wells*

165

Little Raccoon
and the
Thing in the Pool

by
Lilian Moore

Little Raccoon was little

but he was brave.

One day Mother Raccoon said,

"Tonight the moon will be out.

It will be bright and full.

Can you go to the pool

all by yourself, Little Raccoon?

Can you get some fish for supper?"

"Oh, yes, yes!" said Little Raccoon.

"I'll get the best fish you ever ate.

We can bake it for supper."

Little Raccoon was little

but he was brave.

That night the moon came up
big and full and very bright.

"Go now, Little Raccoon,"
said his mother.
"Walk to the pool.
You will see a big tree
that makes a bridge over the pool.
Walk over the pool on the tree.
The best place to get fish
is on the other side."

Little Raccoon went away
in the bright moonlight.

He was very happy!

Here he was walking in the woods
all by himself.

He walked a little.

He ran a little.

And now and then he skipped.

Soon Little Raccoon reached
the place where the big trees were.

There was Old Porcupine.

Old Porcupine was surprised
to see Little Raccoon walking
in the woods without his mother.

"Where are you going,
all by yourself?" asked Old Porcupine.

"To the pool," said Little Raccoon.
"I'm going to get some fish
to bake for supper."

"Be careful, Little Raccoon,"
said Old Porcupine.
"You don't have what I have,
you know!"

"I'm not afraid,"
said Little Raccoon.

He was little but he was brave.

Little Raccoon went on
in the bright moonlight.
He walked a little.
He ran a little.
And now and then he skipped.

Soon he reached the place
where the green grass was.
There was Big Skunk.

Big Skunk was surprised, too,
to see Little Raccoon walking
in the woods without his mother.

"Where are you going,
all by yourself?" asked Big Skunk.

"To the pool," said Little Raccoon.
"I'm going to get some fish
for supper."

"Be careful, Little Raccoon,"
said Big Skunk.
"You don't have what I have,
you know!"

"I'm not afraid,"
said Little Raccoon, and he went on.

Soon he saw Fat Rabbit.

Fat Rabbit was sleeping,
but he opened one eye.

Then he jumped up.

"My, you scared me!" he said.

"Where are you going,
all by yourself, Little Raccoon?"

"I'm going to the pool,"
said Little Raccoon.

"Way over there on the other side
of the pool."

"OOOOOH!" said Fat Rabbit.
"Aren't you afraid of IT?"

"Afraid of what?"
asked Little Raccoon.

"Of the thing in the pool!"
said Fat Rabbit. "I am!"

"I'm not!" said Little Raccoon,
and he went on.

Soon Little Raccoon reached
the big tree that was over the pool.

"This is where I cross,"
said Little Raccoon to himself.

"And over there on the other side
is where I get the fish."

Little Raccoon walked onto the tree
and began to cross the pool.

He was brave, but he did wish
he had not seen Fat Rabbit.

He did not want to think about IT.

He did not want to think
about the thing in the pool.

But he couldn't help it.

He just had to stop and look.

There was something in the pool!

There it was,

in the bright moonlight,

looking up at him!

Little Raccoon did not want it

to know that he was afraid.

He made a face.

The thing in the pool

made a face, too.

And what a mean face it was!

Little Raccoon was scared.

He ran away!

He ran past Fat Rabbit
and scared him.

He ran and ran and did not stop
until he saw Big Skunk.

"What is it? What is it?"
asked Big Skunk.

"There's a big thing in the pool!"
said Little Raccoon.
"I can't get past it!"

"Do you want me to go with you?"
asked Big Skunk.
"I can make it go away."

179

"Oh, no, no!" said Little Raccoon.
"You don't have to do that!"

"Then you'll have to take a rock
with you," said Big Skunk.
"Just show that thing in the pool
that you have a rock!"

Little Raccoon did want
to get some good fish.
He took a rock and walked back
to the pool.

"Maybe the thing went away,"
Little Raccoon said to himself.

But no.

When he looked down into the pool,
there it was!

Little Raccoon did not want to show
that he was afraid.

He let the thing in the pool see
that he had a rock.

But the thing in the pool
had a rock, too.

And what a big rock it was!

Little Raccoon was brave
but he was little.

He ran like anything.

He ran and ran,
and he did not stop
until he saw Old Porcupine.

"What is it? What is it?"
asked Old Porcupine.

Little Raccoon told him
about the thing in the pool.

"He had a rock, too,"
said Little Raccoon.

"A big BIG rock!"

"Then you must have a stick
this time," said Old Porcupine.

"Go back and show that thing
that you have a big stick!"

Little Raccoon did want
to get some good fish.

He took a stick and walked back
to the pool.

"Maybe this time it went away,"
Little Raccoon said to himself.

But no.

The thing in the pool was still there.

Little Raccoon did not wait.

He showed the thing in the pool his big stick.

But the thing in the pool had a stick, too.

A big BIG stick.

Little Raccoon turned and ran.

He ran and ran past Fat Rabbit —

past Big Skunk —

past Old Porcupine —
and he did not stop until he was home.

Little Raccoon told his mother
all about the thing in the pool.

"Oh, Mother," he said,
"I wanted to go for fish
all by myself.

I wanted to get good fish
for supper!"

"And you will!" said Mother Raccoon.
"Go back to the pool, Little Raccoon.
But this time do not make a face.
Do not take a rock.
Do not take a stick."

"But what can I do?"
asked Little Raccoon.

"Just smile," said Mother Raccoon.
"This time just keep smiling
at the thing in the pool."

"Is that all?" asked Little Raccoon.
"Are you sure?"

"That is all," said his mother.
"I am sure."

Little Raccoon was brave,
and his mother was sure!

He went all the way back to the pool.

"Maybe the thing went away at last,"
he said to himself.

But no.

There it was!

Little Raccoon made himself look down
into the pool.

Then he made himself smile
at the thing in the pool.

The thing in the pool smiled back!

Little Raccoon was happy!

He began to laugh.

The thing in the pool began

to laugh, too, just like

a happy raccoon.

"Now it wants to be friends,"

said Little Raccoon to himself.

"Now I can cross!"

And he ran on the tree

to the other side of the pool.

Little Raccoon began to look

for fish in the pool.

Soon he had all the fish he wanted.

He ran back across the pool.

This time Little Raccoon waved

to the thing in the pool.

The thing in the pool waved back!

Little Raccoon went home

with the fish as fast as he could go.

It was the best fish

he and Mother Raccoon ever ate.

"I can go by myself any time,"
said Little Raccoon.

"I'm not afraid of the thing
in the pool now."

"I know," said Mother Raccoon.

"The thing in the pool isn't mean
at all!" said Little Raccoon.

"I know," said Mother Raccoon.

Little Raccoon looked at his mother.
"Tell me," he said.
"What is the thing in the pool?"

Mother Raccoon began to laugh.
Then she told him.

More Than One Meaning

You know that a word can have more than one meaning.

The other words in the sentence will help you think of the right meaning.

Look at the picture.

Here are two sentences.

1. There isn't **room** for one more animal.

2. I have many toy animals in my **room.**

Can you find the sentence that goes with the picture?

Can you find the right sentences

for the pictures here?

1. My little sister **waves** to me

when I come home from school.

2. The **waves** made a big noise

as they banged into the rocks.

1. I will **show** you how to fish.

2. We are having a dog **show.**

Can you find the right sentences

for the pictures here?

1. Can you **play** with me after school?

2. They are having a **play**

about three billy goats.

1. I am a **mean** troll!

2. I didn't **mean** to fall asleep.

OFF FOR A HIKE

My puppy can't speak English,
she doesn't know a letter,
but her wiggles and her wriggles
when she sees me get my sweater
and her raggle-taggle waggles
when I pack a lunch and pet her
are just as good as talking is . . .
and maybe even better.

—Aileen Fisher

Find the Animals

There are animals hiding

in this picture.

Can you find them?

Did you find a raccoon and a squirrel?

Did you find a porcupine,

two chipmunks,

and——

three little skunks?

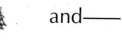

COOKIES

by Arnold Lobel

oad baked some cookies.

"These cookies smell very good,"
said Toad.

He ate one.

"And they taste even better,"
he said.

Toad ran to Frog's house.

"Frog, Frog," cried Toad,

"taste these cookies that I have made."

Frog ate one of the cookies.

"These are the best cookies
I have ever eaten!" said Frog.

Frog and Toad ate many cookies,
one after another.

"You know, Toad," said Frog,
with his mouth full,
"I think we should stop eating.
We will soon be sick."

"You are right," said Toad.

"Let us eat one last cookie,
and then we will stop."

Frog and Toad ate one last cookie.

There were many cookies
left in the bowl.

"Frog," said Toad, "let us eat one very last cookie, and then we will stop."

Frog and Toad ate one very last cookie.

"We must stop eating!" cried Toad as he ate another.

"Yes," said Frog, reaching for a cookie, "we need will power."

"What is will power?" asked Toad.

"**W**ill power is trying hard <u>not</u> to do something that you really want to do," said Frog.

"You mean like trying <u>not</u> to eat all of these cookies?" asked Toad.

"Right," said Frog.

Frog put the cookies in a box.

"There," he said.

"Now we will not eat
any more cookies."

"But we can open the box,"
said Toad.

"That is true," said Frog.

Frog tied some string
around the box.

"There," he said.

"Now we will not eat
any more cookies."

"But we can cut the string
and open the box," said Toad.

"That is true," said Frog.

Frog got a ladder.

He put the box up on a high shelf.

"There," said Frog.

"Now we will not eat
any more cookies."

"But we can climb the ladder
and take the box down from the shelf
and cut the string and open the box,"
said Toad.

"That is true,"
said Frog.

Frog climbed the ladder
and took the box down from the shelf.

He cut the string and opened the box.

rog took the box outside.

He shouted in a loud voice,

"HEY BIRDS, HERE ARE COOKIES!"

Birds came from everywhere.

They picked up all the cookies

in their beaks and flew away.

"Now we have no more cookies
to eat," said Toad sadly.

"Not even one."

"Yes," said Frog,
"but we have lots and lots
of will power."

"You may keep it all, Frog,"
said Toad.

"I am going home now to bake a cake."

CDEFGHIJ-D-843210/7987